God's Vision or Television?

How Television Influences What We Believe

This book is dedicated to my mother,
Lottie M. Wright,
and my children,
Stephen, Amanda, and Natalie.

God's Vision or Television?

How Television Influences What We Believe

Urban Ministries, Inc.
The African American Christian Publishing
& Communications Co.

CARL JEFFREY WRIGHT

Urban Ministries, Inc.
The African American Christian Publishing
& Communications Co.

Publisher UMI (Urban Ministries, Inc.)
P. O. Box 436987
Chicago, IL 60643-6987
1-800-860-8642
www.urbanministries.com

Unless otherwise indicated, all Scripture references are taken from the authorized King
James Version of the Bible.

ISBN 0-940955-90-3

Printed in the United States of America.

Table of Contents

Acknowledgments

This book is possible because of the dedication and hard work of Dr. Melvin Banks, chairman and founder, and my colleagues at UMI:

Karla Addison
Endon Anderson
Harriett Barry
Megan Bell
Carla Branch
Shawan Brand
Latricia Bray
Cheryl Brinston
Kim Brooks
Patricia Brooks
Evangeline Carey
Darryl Carlisle
Aja Carr
Rita Clanton
Terrance Clark
Darcy Dalrymple
Quiana Dockery
Odell Fugate
Debbie Gray
Kathryn Hall
Terri Hannett
Zina Harris
Monique Hill
Dr. Judy Hull

Marlin Jamison
Don Jarka
James King
William Martin
Jennifer McIntyre
Hattie Meeks
Melvin Mullins
Drusie Neal
Ken Patel
Kim Pollard
Tiphany Pugh
Dorothy Reasonova
Charon Ross
Kathy Steward
Jason Stewart
Joann Scaife
Katara Washington
Lori Welton
Shalanda White
Leshia Williams
Sandra Williams
Cheryl Wilson
Ken Wolgemuth
Trinidad Zavala

*Special thanks to the Editorial team (names in bold)
I also wish to thank Larry Taylor Design, Ltd. For the design, cover, and layout of this book; Denise Gates for copyediting and proofreading; Elayne Marchbanks for her invaluable assistance in the completion of this work; and Lakita Garth, who gave me many valuable comments and insights.

Preface

Purpose of the Book. This book was developed specifically to be used with the church-wide Bible study course, *Spotlight on Jesus!* Jesus said in John 8:12, (NIV) *"I am the light of the world. Whoever follows me will never walk in darkness, but will have the light of life."*

Why This Course Was Chosen. This course was developed on the solid foundation of teaching the basic beliefs of the Christian faith. For 2004, the spotlight is on Jesus and how we can exemplify Him in our lives. Jesus is the ultimate role model and as His followers, we need to study His life and purpose so that we can walk in obedience and follow His example. In these troubling times, people young and old need to know more than ever that Jesus is the light of the world and what believing in Jesus is all about.

For that reason, *Spotlight on Jesus!* is all about Jesus and how to build faith in Him.

The Leader's Guide. A separate leader's guide accompanies the book. It is designed to assist those who lead groups where this book is used as a text. Each chapter of the leader guide contains a suggested lesson plan, with small group activities described in detail. It also contains answers to the Bible study application questions contained in the related student workbook.

The Student Workbook. A separate student workbook accompanies the student book. Each chapter contains an in-depth Bible study application. The application consists of five Bible discovery exercises, a church ministry application question, and a personal application question.

It is our hope that after reading this book you will never watch television the same way again.

Introduction

Television is influential. In the United States, it is the main thing we do—and we do a lot of it. The average American sits in front of the screen *watching* TV for what amounts to one entire day (about 20 hours per week) (Peers 2004, B1). As Americans, we are different for many reasons, but the habitual viewing of television is probably what separates us from most of the people in the world today. We rely on television for our vision. One writer has defined vision as "a clear mental image of *what could be,* fueled by the conviction that *it should be*" (Stanley 2001, 18). Vision, in America, comes from television. Television has given us a vision, and we believe in it.

Americans spend more time getting their visions from television than any other people in the world, and African Americans watch more of it than anyone else. We spend many more hours a week watching this medium than the average American, and its impact on our vision has been devastating. The televising of certain aspects of African American culture, a relatively recent phenomena, has changed the world's youth culture. The words, *urban, hip-hop,* and *bling, bling* define the music, dress, and lifestyle of teens and young adults across racial and geographic boundaries. Unfortunately, this vision, or televised lifestyle, includes far more violence, drugs, sex, and vulgar language than most people would care to see expressed in our youth.

Ironically, religious television, including African American preaching programs, has had nearly as much additional exposure for about the same length of time as the music and rap videos that so many complain about. The growth of cable and satellite television has produced more religious programming than ever. The major impact of these religious shows seems to be the multiplication of religious television shows, but no visible difference in the culture. The religion of materialism and consumption has developed to the highest degree in human history through television.

In some instances the message of acquisitive consumerism that is communicated through the prosperous lifestyles, luxurious cars, expensive clothes, and flashy jewelry of television's preachers is exactly the same as the music video stars. But the music videos have better beats and seem to get more converts. Actually, it is sometimes difficult to tell the difference between the two because regardless of whether they are preaching or rapping, what we see is the same: the accumulation and display of wealth, conspicuous consumption, and a lifestyle that suggests that the goal of life is to create the highest amount of comfort before death comes.

Though it is not a specific focus of this book, television's influence on politics has been most profound. We now choose virtually all key elected officials based primarily on what they look like on television and how much money they spend on television advertising. In the presidential election of 2000, the candidates so closely resembled each other that for White Americans it was a virtual tie. African Americans could only distinguish the two candidates by the labels they wore; because television has taught us that Republicans are racists and Democrats are not, we had a basis for choice other than appearance.

The irony of this is that ideologically, African Americans have far more in common with Republicans than Democrats.

According to author Neil Postman, this is a world where "discourse is conducted largely through visual imagery, which is to say that television gives us a conversation in images not words" (1985). The fact is that African American beliefs about morality, school choice, crime, big government, and other political platform issues are largely Republican. This is completely overwhelmed by the vision of a pickup truck dragging a Black man or a Black male athlete going to jail for having sex with a White woman, while a White corporate executive pays a $5 million bail to go home after being charged with looting billions of dollars from millions of people. Racism produces unforgettable imagery and the visual lifestyle differences that result from it overwhelm all other political ideas.

The influence of television news is unquestioned. Although the news habit is purely a function of technology and there is no single set of important events that occurs each day that we all need to know about, television has led us to believe that a person who has not watched the news is an uninformed and unintelligent person. The news habit is a creation of the technology; it's a media event. There is no news of the day in cultures that are not trapped by television. The point here is not that important things do not happen, but rather that the decision about what is important and the process by which you get this information is not the product of some quest for absolute truth but simply another way to get you to watch television. A lot of "important" things that happened were not on the news, like the half billion new Christians in Africa and the shift of Christianity from the White Western World to the "Brown" Southern Hemisphere.

The total purpose of television is entertainment. The goal—to sell you products.

Television has become dominated by a few very large conglomerates that have now acquired control of virtually all media. By media we mean the means of communicating information or entertainment to large audiences at the same time. The various forms include newspapers, magazines, books, television programs, movies, music, and digital versions of these forms, which can be contained on various types of objects such as CDs or DVDs and can also be made directly available over the Internet (so-called "e-content").

The corporations that bring you this content have as their overriding purpose the goal of "increasing shareholder value." They want to grow larger and more profitable because that increases the value of the company and creates wealth for management and for the people who own stock in them. It does not matter whether the show is good or bad in any moral sense of the word. The only question is: Does it attract and retain viewers so that commercials can be sold for more money?

As a consequence, much of television today is of very low moral value, though the economic value is high. The most highly watched television programs, the Super Bowl, the Oscars, the Grammy Awards, the final episodes of *Sex and the City* and *Friends,* all offer very little, if any, redeeming moral content. But the many millions spent for 30 and 60 second commercials during these programs shows that they have tremendous value to the companies that own them.

Through television, the country today has exalted "free market capitalism" as its highest value. With a very few exceptions, primarily illegal drugs, it is OK to sell anything in the U.S. The law of the market has superceded biblical law, which is the actual root of law in Western society. The nation has evolved, or perhaps devolved, to a non-moral based system that protects not the good of society or the development of health and respect for the individual, but rather protects the right to make money.

This protection has meant that government regulation of the use of the airwaves and the content of television has been ineffective, except in the most minimal of ways. Anything can be shown and is being shown. The president of Viacom appeared before Congress after his company's televised half-time sex show at the 2004 Super Bowl and stated that while he felt the show was inappropriate and possibly offensive, it probably was not *illegal* under the vague decency standards of the FCC. The consequences for society and its children are that parents have to protect them or they have to fend for themselves.

The result is increased violence, drug use, alcoholism, suicide, and perverted and extramarital sexual activity. The definition of "free speech" and the "rights" of people and companies has been stretched to include behavior that in another time would have been prosecuted.

Black people and other minorities have been victimized personally by the visual stereotypes that make them poster children for the most negative aspects of behavior and lifestyle in programming, music videos, and television news. This follows a centuries old belief system in Western/European/American philosophy and thought that evolutionary hierarchy of man begins with Europeans and descends to various people of color with Africans at the lowest level of humanity—and animals not far behind. Reinforcing this social mythology through television programs and films that depict a reality that supports this view has been the most insidious effect of television on Black people.

What all Christians, Black or White, should be doing is supporting the explosion of Christianity in the Southern Hemisphere and addressing the AIDS crisis here and in Africa. This is a divine vision for the entire church and a mandate for the Black church. Paul boldly wrote, "if any provide not for his own, ...he... is worse than an infidel" (1 Timothy 5:8, KJV). Isn't the Black church called to address the needs of the church in Africa, and what about the millions of AIDS orphans there? African Americans have annual household incomes of nearly $700 billion, more than all the Black population of Africa combined. While it is true that we have many problems here, our vision should also include helping those who were left behind. Why do we need a television special to tell us this is a serious problem that needs to be addressed? We must redirect our time and attention to the vision that God has put before us.

In the chapters that follow, we will address ten issues comparing the worldview of television with that of the Bible. As you explore the material, you will be challenged to consider new ways of thinking and to develop new habits of watching, or not watching. It is my hope that you choose God's vision, not television.

CHAPTER ONE

TELEVISION–Is What You See Really What You Get?

GOD'S WORD REVEALS GOD'S PLAN

The Bible reports that God came to earth in human form. He did this according to a plan that was conceived before the beginning of time and unfolded through human history. The plan included the family (the Jews), the place, and the circumstances—a virgin birth that would leave no doubt that this was God's doing. Abraham and his descendants have the distinction of being the family that God chose for His entry into humanity. Bethlehem was the place; it is a land we still call the Holy Land. Mary, the great-granddaughter of Abraham, was the virgin chosen to give birth to God in the flesh. God's purpose? To rescue mankind from its own evil by offering the atoning blood of a substitute, Jesus Christ, God Himself, to pay the penalty of death so that we can have the gift of eternal life. This is the basic story of the Bible.

TELEVISION IS UNBELIEVABLE, BUT WE BELIEVE IT

TV Guide gives the listings of television shows for the week. It tells us that "The Sopranos" will be on HBO at 8:00 p.m. on Sunday. Turn on the television at that time and there it is. We believe it because it happened. A brief synopsis of the show describes the plot of the night's episode. Sure enough, that is what the show is about. We don't consider for a second that it might be about something else.

The Old Testament book of Micah foretold that Bethlehem would be the place that Jesus would be born (Micah 5:2). Isaiah 7:14 foretold that the birth would be to a virgin. Matthew 1:20 recounts the angels' visit to explain these Old Testament Scriptures to Joseph so he would not put his wife away, thinking that she was pregnant by another man. If, like Joseph, angels appeared to us to confirm the things in the Bible, perhaps we would believe all of it too. But we readily believe most of what we see on TV news and rarely, if ever, do we question it.

TELEVISION, A RELIABLE SOURCE?

We get more information from television than virtually every other media source. According to the *Wall Street Journal*, most people watch an average of 20 hours of television a week compared to time spent reading newspapers, magazines, or books, which averages about 2-3 hours per week (see appendix A). Time spent in church, prayer, or Bible reading doesn't even compare since most people spend approximately 3 hours or less there as well. Unfortunately, statistics show that African Americans watch even more television. At the same time, Nielsen research reports that African Americans watch as much as 30 or more hours of television per week (see appendix C, Nielsen website). In addition, studies show that getting news from cable television is the primary source for more than half the people in the country, ahead of newspapers, local television news, and network television combined (Jones 2002).[1] However, there has never been a worse time in history to rely on television for information. Instead of reporting the truth, television has resorted to simply providing *infotainment*.

HOW DO WE KNOW WHAT IS TRUE?

News on television never has been very good. The broadcasts are short, lasting only 22 minutes. Stories are rarely more than a minute or two and details are few. The viewer doesn't get to ask clarifying questions and the broadcasts move so quickly that they are on to the next story before a question can even come to mind. You might hear about a spacecraft exploding and killing seven people but it would take a lot more than the nightly news to explain why they were risking their lives going into space in the first place, what the goals were, and what went wrong. As the authors of *It Ain't Necessarily So* put it, "the news clearly has a relationship to the truth, but it is never simply equivalent to it" (Murray 2002, 6).

If God's plan ever made the news, the thing most likely to be reported about the Mary and Joseph scandal would be the virgin birth, not the historical promise of God that was finally and miraculously fulfilled—and definitely not the angel's encounter with Joseph (after all, that was a dream). They could have a medical examiner and some scientist confirm that Mary was a virgin. However, Joseph's dreams are not likely to make the news no matter how interesting or significant they were. Then if we did not live in the Bethlehem area, we would not see the story anyway. The international news we receive is only a fraction of what really occurs.

THE GOAL OF TELEVISION REVEALED

There is a simple explanation for this. The primary goal of a television show is to attract viewers so that advertising can be sold and broadcasters and production companies can make money. I remember growing up marveling that television was *free*. Just buy a television, turn it on, and there were lots of free things to watch. But the reality is that television is not free at all. The people who pay for television ads know that they will make money by getting you to buy the things they advertise. Television broadcasters and production companies make programs that will attract people who want to spend money so that they can sell those commercials for the highest price possible. Everyone understands that Super Bowl commercials are the most expensive because the most people are watching. It is all about money—you knew that. Why else would they spend almost two and a half million dollars on a thirty-second ad?

What you may not have known, though, is just how much money there is and how few people are getting it. Five companies control television today: Time Warner, Disney, Viacom, News Corporation, and General Electric. This is actually an improvement from when it was just three companies in the past. The companies that control television got their start in radio and then graduated to television when it was invented and became more profitable than radio. Two of these companies that dominate television also still have significant control over radio news today. Disney and Viacom and just two other companies control two thirds of the news radio in America today (McChesney and Nichols 2002, 48-49).[2]

CONSOLIDATION IN MEDIA

Over the last 20 years, tremendous consolidation has occurred in virtually all forms of media. Ten global firms dominate the major forms of media (newspapers, books, film, television, radio, and recorded music). A closer look at the three largest firms gives a clear picture of how much concentration exists in the industry. For example, Time Warner owns CNN, the WB Network, HBO, the Cartoon Network, Warner Brothers Pictures, Warner Brothers Television, New Line Cinema, the largest magazine publishing group, which includes *Time, Fortune, Sports Illustrated, Entertainment Weekly, People,* and a half interest in *Essence Magazine.* And these are only a few of what Time Warner owns. Time Warner's chairman, Richard Parsons, is African American, and probably produces more media content than any other firm with its huge library of films, TV shows, music, books, and cartoons.

Disney is close to Time Warner in size and has a similar global reach. Disney has evolved from a theme park and animated movie company into a media empire that includes ABC Network, ESPN, The Disney Channel, ABC Family, and ownership interests in A&E, E! Entertainment, The History Channel, and Lifetime. Disney film studios include Miramax and Touchstone in addition to Walt Disney Pictures, which allows the same company that brings you *Snow White* to give you *Pulp Fiction*. Other Disney companies include Hyperion Books and a substantial music business. All this and theme parks, too. These are only a few of the companies that Disney owns. As this book is being written, Disney is currently the subject of a takeover proposal by Comcast, the largest cable operator in the country. This merger, if it occurs, would create the largest media conglomerate of all.

News Corporation, headed by Rupert Murdoch, is not the largest company but has an incredible global presence in media markets with a particularly strong presence in the U.S. In addition to the Fox Broadcasting Company, News Corporation owns 22 television stations covering 40 percent of the U.S. population; the Fox News Channel; Fox Sports Net; the National Geographic Channel, 130 daily newspapers, including the *New York Post*, the *Times* (of London), and the leading Australian newspapers, to name only a few. News Corporation just recently acquired DIRECTV, the largest U.S. satellite service with 12 million subscribers, which combined with its existing holdings, give it satellite broadcasting capacity on five continents. The company also owns leading book publisher, HarperCollins, which is the parent company of Zondervan, the largest publisher of the widely read *New International Version* of the Bible (see appendix B).

WHAT THIS MEANS FOR TRUTH

With this kind of concentration in media, a balanced understanding of the world events cannot be gained from television alone. This is especially true for news of events that threaten the corporate control of the companies that dominate media. In 2003, when the Federal Communications

Commission proposed several changes that would increase the number of television stations that a company could own, there was virtually no coverage of this on television news. Rules that currently prevent the media companies that control television from buying newspapers in the same markets they serve were also considered for repeal. These events have been the subject of very limited public discussion or debate.

Christians need to be particularly sensitive to issues of media concentration. As we will discuss later in this book, the worldview of television stands in virtual opposition to the worldview of the Christian. No Christian can afford to live their life using television as their sole source or even as their primary source of information and opinion. To quote David Murray from *It Ain't Necessarily So:* "Until we learn the intricacies of the media culture and the processes by which news is made, we are vulnerable to a daily dose of misunderstanding contained in each morning's headlines" (p.1). Both newspapers and television have been shown to favor negative stories over positive ones, liberal bias over conservative, and criticism over positive social commentary. There is virtually no coverage of the church or spiritual matters unless it involves some scandal like a pedophile priest.

WHAT YOU NEED TO CONSIDER

Guard your faith from falsehood by weighing every opinion against the Word of God. The latest opinion polls, the views of Oprah Winfrey, the commentators on Fox News, or even the "man on the street" reactions from 60 Minutes, must line up with the Word of God or be rejected. Which opinion carries more weight, Dan Rather's or the apostle

Paul's? It is easy to be convinced that "everybody" is doing "it" from one television show or newscast when in fact nobody is doing it but the people on the show. The founders of MTV, for example, were very explicit in defining their aim as shifting youth culture, not just reflecting it or marketing to it.

AFRICAN AMERICANS NEED TO BE ESPECIALLY CAREFUL ABOUT TELEVISION

So little of true African American life is reflected in television. This is not just a result of too few Blacks in leadership roles in the industry; it is done in spite of the fact that Blacks watch more television—a lot more. Nielsen Media reports that African Americans over 50 are watching nine and one half hours of daytime television compared to about five hours and twenty minutes for everyone else (see appendix C, Nielsen web site). That is almost twice as much! It has long been a complaint of the African American community that the few images of athletes, comedians, criminals, and entertainers do not adequately reflect the fullness of African American life. The media conglomerates—who own BET, by the way (Viacom purchased the cable channel in 2001)— have little economic incentive to program positive images of African Americans because relatively few African Americans make up the target audience of consumers that they are trying to reach.

EVERYONE NEEDS TO WATCH LESS AND READ MORE

The more television you watch, the more susceptible you are to its influence. Even though the same media giants control much of book publishing, there are still many independent publishers and many, many web sites that offer alternative viewpoints and a Christian worldview on contemporary events. The U.S. is quickly evolving into a nation that can be divided between those who watch and those who read. Christians should seek to stay as long as possible on the side of the readers, beginning with increased Bible reading. Although Christian television provides some alternatives, the majority of what is available on television today will not pass the test of 1 Corinthians 10:31, (NLT): "whatever you do, you must do all for the glory of God." The two hours a week that most people spend in worship or Bible study will not hold up against the 20 hours of television watching that we do.

BUYING LESS RESULTS FROM WATCHING LESS TELEVISION

When you understand that television is designed to create a desire and demand for more by making you dissatisfied with what you have, you will watch less television and buy fewer things that you probably do not need. Instead of violating "thou shalt not covet," we should consider possessing the joy of contentment (Exodus 20:17; 1 Timothy 6:6, KJV).

CHAPTER TWO

TELEVISION—God's Promises and TV's Promises

GOD'S PROMISES TO US

The Bible records hundreds of promises that God made to us. The big one is that forgiveness for the things we have done wrong and the reward of a life lived perfectly is ours for the asking. This is all possible because God promised that when He came to earth, He was coming to fulfill His promise to Abraham. The promise to Abraham was not simply the West Bank of the Jordan. The promise was that Abraham's descendants and all the nations of the earth would be blessed through him. God's greatest promise to man was the promise of a Messiah, a Savior, who would once and for all bring man into a right relationship with God. It was a promise God kept.

In the Gospel of Luke, the Bible story opens with God keeping His promise of the Messiah's birth. The story begins with the parents of John the Baptist, Zechariah and Elizabeth. They heard from an angel that after years of praying for a child, Elizabeth was pregnant with John. The names "Zechariah" and "Elizabeth" taken together mean, "God remembers." Their son would become the greatest evangelist that had ever lived according to the words of Christ (Matthew 11:11). John was a man with a singular message that the people should change their hearts and their behavior and prepare for the coming of the Messiah, the Christ. Elizabeth is visited by the pregnant Virgin Mary and confirms for Mary the blessing of being chosen by God for this sacred birth. After Jesus was born and taken to the temple for His baby blessing, two more witnesses, Simeon and Anna, give further confirmation that this Child is indeed the fulfillment of God's promise. Once again, God kept His promise.

TELEVISION'S PROMISES

The promises of television are sometimes subtle and other times direct, but they are rarely kept. Advertising promises that if you drink a certain beer, beautiful women will show up and want to return to your apartment; a shampoo will cause men to want to take you out and worship you like a goddess; and a toy that doesn't have batteries will evoke thoughts of movie soundtracks that are so loud and realistic that the child will hear them when he or she plays with that toy. Concrete playgrounds are transformed into realistic western landscapes. Little girls will be able to bring plastic dolls to life and be "just like mommy." The promises that television has woven through images presented over the years, have become more and more compelling.

Advertising has been designed to produce consumption to

get you to buy, use, and buy again. Billions are spent on commercials that make the promise that things you eat, wear, and own will make you feel better and satisfy the desires of your heart. Cigarettes, which poison the lungs and body, promised cool satisfaction until the evidence of that broken promise was so clear that television advertising was banned. But the advertisers figured out that placing the products in the hands of popular actors in TV shows was an even more compelling way to make the promise that smoking was cool and would make you look better and feel better.

NEUROMARKETING: MAKING YOU BELIEVE THE PROMISE

Because so few of the promises are true, advertisers have had to increase their sophistication in developing approaches to make consumers buy their products. In the early days of television, testimonials were common. "I used Brand X and the results were terrible. I switched to Bling! and now my clothes are cleaner." From anonymous actors to celebrities, the power of advertising's promises increased although often the products couldn't deliver. Unlike God, whose Word is true (Numbers 23:19), advertisers' promises are empty and broken.

Neuromarketing is being evaluated in experiments where they are searching to find the "buy button inside the skull" or that place in the brain that really makes you want to buy something (Wells 2003, 62-70). At Emory University, neuromarketing research is using "magnetic resonance imaging" (MRI) to identify patterns of brain activity that reveal how a person responds to television advertising and using these findings to develop more effective ads. The goal is to get customers to behave the way advertisers want them to behave (see appendix C, Commercial Alert web site).

THE PROBLEM OF EXCESSIVE CONSUMPTION

At the root of this need for more effective promises to generate increased consumption is an insatiable appetite for corporate growth. Expanding the list of things we "need" and "must have" has been a strategy for corporate growth that has been more effectively executed through television programming and commercials than almost any other medium. Television convinces viewers that the latest kitchen gadget, exercise equipment, skin treatment program, car, electronic device, or computer is a necessity. As a result, we are always dissatisfied or unhappy with what we have, and completely at odds with the Scriptures that encourage us to seek contentment (Philippians 4:11-13; 1 Timothy 6:6-10).

The use and abuse of credit cards over the last 20 years has boosted the economy but has also produced waste and excess consumption. But despite all this credit card debt, many Americans still do not have the basics of a healthy diet, housing, clothing, and health care. In a consumer credit report, the Federal Reserve reported that total consumer debt exceeded $2 trillion as of November 2003, an amount that is nearly $20,000 per U.S. household. This is double the average amount of credit card debt and car loans people had 10 years ago, excluding home mortgages (see appendix C, Federal Reserve web site).

The results of excess consumption are not surprising. The savings rate is less than 2 percent after tax income, making many people just one paycheck away from being flat broke. In addition, the American Bankruptcy Institute reports that bankruptcies are at an all-time high with over 1.5 million bankruptcies declared in 2002 (see appendix C, ABI web site). Yet the shopping goes on. With increased consumer debt, there is a corresponding increase in bankruptcy filings. People spend with a sense of entitlement and with virtually no sense of the importance of limiting consumption or helping others. They repeatedly believe the false promise that another purchase will provide satisfaction. In doing so, they miss the true blessing that can only come from a life of contentment in Christ.

WHAT YOU NEED TO CONSIDER

Seeking contentment over consumption is the key to defeating this advertising-generated malady. Many have had the experience of wanting something so badly, only to find that after getting it the feeling did not last. Affluenza describes the condition where you feel you must always have more to be satisfied and content. Often the only pleasure that comes from the new purchase is the pleasure of showing it off to someone else who wants it. If you are buying things just to show them to others—if you have a garage, basement, or closet full of unused items that you bought but haven't touched since you brought them home—you might have affluenza. Sell it, give it away, or throw it away, and stop the buying. Try buying just essential food and clothing for a year, only replacing items that you need for daily existence. For example, a can opener might qualify but not that new copy of your favorite DVD.

Since African Americans watch more television, it is no surprise that in many product categories African Americans are the heaviest consumers. Given this phenomenon, African Americans should strive to avoid overconsumption and instead focus on wealth creation. According to market research, African Americans are dominant buyers of products in categories such as personal care, gifts, women's apparel, and footwear (see appendix C, Target Market News web site). The sad result of excessive consumption is that it prevents the creation of wealth (defined as a positive net worth) when the value of the amount you own exceeds the amount you owe. The Scriptures tell us that we should leave an inheritance to our children's children (Proverbs 13:22). However, too many African Americans cannot leave an inheritance because the money was spent on a big-screen TV or spinning rims for an SUV.

Focusing on self instead of others, especially the poor, is a direct result of the television induced, self-centered consumption that always makes you number one. The sin of Sodom and Gomorrah was not merely sexual impurity as is often thought, but also "pride, laziness, and gluttony, while the poor and needy suffered outside her door" (Ezekiel 16:49, NLT) resulting in their destruction. African Americans find themselves in the richest nation on the planet with annual incomes of nearly three quarters of a trillion dollars. This is more than the combined income of nearly all the other people of African descent worldwide. The Bible says: "much is required from those to whom much is given" (Luke 12:48, NLT). Is God looking for African Americans to rise to a new level of giving to assist Africa and other poor people of African descent around the world? Could your church be doing more in genuine missions outreach?

Make your promises good and commit to changed behavior before the neuromarketers make the change for you. You can change someone's life by keeping your promises. If you are guilty of overconsumption, too much debt, too much television, or too little concern for the poor, make a promise to change now and keep it.

CHAPTER THREE

TELEVISION—
Miracles and
Ministry

THE HEALING MINISTRY OF JESUS

The power of Christianity rests in the deity of Jesus Christ; without this truth it would simply be just another religion. Jesus proved He was the Messiah through the fulfillment of many prophecies and through His own foretelling of future events. These events, such as the Resurrection, showed His divine authority when they actually came to pass. But the proof that undoubtedly got most of the attention in Jesus' time on earth were the miracles He performed. Disease and sickness were a serious matter during biblical times. Illnesses that are preventable today by proper hygiene or refrigeration of food were deadly during the time of Christ. A man who could heal and raise the dead was surely from God, or as He claimed, was God.

The Gospel of Mark is written almost like a news story would be written today. Chapter 5 records three dramatic instances of healing that particularly stand out. In the first instance, Jesus healed a demon-possessed man who lived in a cemetery and had unusual strength. A large crowd witnessed this event, including many who were very familiar with this man's condition. Mark then reports that after Jesus healed the man, He got into a boat, crossed the lake, and encountered one of the rulers of the synagogue who sought out Jesus to heal his sick daughter. The religious rulers of the day were some of Jesus' greatest opponents. But because Jairus believed Jesus could heal his daughter, he was willing to seek help, even from an "enemy."

Jesus is on His way to heal the man's daughter when the second healing takes place. This time, a woman who believes Jesus can heal her hemorrhaging reaches out in the crowd and touches His coat. She gets healed but her identity is exposed by Jesus. Jesus realized he had been touched and confronts the crowd with the question, "Who touched my clothes?" After the woman identifies herself, Jesus acknowledges that her faith brought about her healing. Jesus then goes on to the synagogue ruler's house where He raises the ruler's daughter from the dead. In this one chapter, Jesus performs three miraculous healings of a man, a woman, and a child before crowds of lots of witnesses in three different settings in the country, in the middle of a crowd, and in the home of a public figure. Is it any wonder that the words and ministry of Jesus are spoken of to this day?

TELEVISION AND MIRACLES

Through the use of special effects, the miraculous seems ordinary on television and in movies today. Jesus' ministry demonstrated His supernatural power in an era before film and TV made these visual phenomena "ordinary" through unbelievable special effects. From "Bewitched" in the 1960s to the special effects of the "X-Files" in the 1990s, many programs depict miraculous occurrences usually associated with demonic forces.

Healing in particular has been the focus of many television ministries, and healing services are commonplace in many churches around the country today. Some have fraudulently used television to re-create these miraculous events and confuse or defraud people for economic gain or other benefits. Jesus Himself foretold that this would occur. While surely God is able to manifest supernatural outcomes today, the misuse of the miraculous has caused much confusion inside and outside the church. The magnitude of the problem has led to the creation of several groups whose purposes are to expose cults, reveal fraud by television evangelists, and help the victims (see appendix C, Personal Freedom Outreach web site).

According to the Trinity Foundation, estimates show that the televangelist donor poll is 5 million people. Of these, 55 percent are elderly and 35 percent are from the poorest and neediest segments of society, who experience the worst kind of suffering, such as those with children suffering from AIDS or spouses suffering from cancer. Only ten percent are from the upper middle-class—people who typically are educated and career-driven are generally the least likely to resort to seeking help from televised faith healers (Anthony 1994).

Ministries that use persuasive promises of a cure or some other financial blessing to encourage people to give money or assets are proliferating again after the lull that followed the scandals of the 1980s. One of the most notorious was that of Jim Bakker, who served a five-year prison sentence for fraudulent activities carried out in his television ministry. Described as one of the primary propagator(s) of the prosperity message in the 20th century, Bakker has since written a book entitled, *I Was Wrong*, disavowing his former prosperity teachings.

WHAT IS WRONG WITH RELIGIOUS TELEVISION?

Apart from false healing services on television, religious programs on television are commonly criticized for five things: (1) the shows are superficial and not doctrinally detailed enough; (2) televangelism promotes values that may contradict traditional Christian values; (3) televangelism is ineffective in reaching nonbelievers; (4) televangelism creates personality cults around the preachers as "stars"; and (5) many televangelists are primarily concerned with money and will use false healing miracles or anything else to get it (Newman 1996, 84-96).

Obviously, there are television ministries being broadcast today that provide examples, which support all of these criticisms. However, it can also be argued that these criticisms are insufficient to support generalization that covers the full range of religious television programs. I believe the problem with religious television, as we most commonly encounter it, is one of boredom and lack of creativity. Too many programs simply talk about or preach about the power of God without demonstrating it in a story, dramatization, animation, or using some of the other techniques and tools available for communication in the television medium. Simply put, there is just too much preaching!

People reaching out to lay hands on their TVs after hearing an invitation from a televangelist is an image that appeals much more to the believer than the unsaved. A more effective use of the medium would be to reenact the stories as opposed to the presentation of service after service and sermon after sermon focused on *telling* the story. Using the power of television could be the best opportunity to reach the lost. A good example of this exists in radio, where dramatizations of Bible stories often have greater impact than sermons that you watch and hear being preached. Jesus used parables in this same way.

WHAT YOU NEED TO CONSIDER

Some secular television programs may be effective at communicating moral truth. While clearly more common in the television of the 60s and early 70s, programming where good wins over evil or an obvious moral emerges from the resolution of conflict can still be found on television. One of the benefits of cable and satellite programming is that many of these older shows are now back on the air as TV Land and other networks recycle the television programs of the past. Unfortunately for African Americans, many of these shows reflect White cultural supremacy and have no Black characters at all. Nevertheless, old episodes of programs like "Andy Griffith" could provide more of an object lesson than an hour of some televangelists' preaching.

Your church's television ministry may need to be transformed into something else. Other formats such as interviews, talk shows, and local news of spiritual significance could be just as cost-efficient and easy to produce as the typical image of the preacher in the pulpit that so predominates today. For many ministries, adequate resources to experiment with different television formats could produce the possibility of multiple program offerings. Using different methods to communicate the message of the Gospel via television is a challenge that must be met by the church today as it seeks to reach ever-larger numbers of visually-oriented, television-trained youth and adults.

Radio and tape ministries also offer opportunity to experiment with new formats. The variety of presenting audio drama, using storytelling, interviews, and other approaches to media content could revitalize a ministry. Just as the early days of television borrowed heavily and often directly from the programs of radio, your church's tape or radio ministry is a potential proving ground for a future television ministry.

CHAPTER FOUR

TELEVISION— Salvation and Love

GOD'S LOVE MANIFESTED IN SALVATION

In his letter to the Philippian Christians, Paul writes that God laid aside His mighty power and glory and "took the humble position of a slave and appeared in human form. And in human form he obediently humbled himself even further by dying a criminal's death on a cross" (Philippians 2:7-8, NLT). Why would God do it? It seems unlikely if any of us were God that we would even consider such humiliation, much less giving up the power even temporarily. What the Bible makes clear is that God did it because of His love for us; a love that would sacrifice in order to restore people to a position of eternal fellowship with God (1 John 4:9-10). God did it out of a love that exceeds the bounds of human capacity to love (Romans 5:8-11).

In a late night conversation with the Jewish ruling council member Nicodemus, Jesus explains that God loved the world so much that He sent His Son into the world to save the world. In what may be the most quoted and memorized verse in the Bible, John 3:16, Jesus shares that this love of God was intended to give us eternal life. This love is then contrasted with condemnation and is received and rooted in belief—an act of will that requires neither money nor acts of sacrifice, but rather simply accepting and receiving the love given by God. God's love is continually forgiving and open to restoration of man to God (1 John 1:9). It is a love so perfect that its very definition is God Himself, and the Bible explains in 1 John 4:8 (KJV) that "God is love."

LOVE, A MAJOR THEME OF TELEVISION

In the world of television, love also triumphs. *The Love Boat, The Newlywed Game, The Bachelor,* and *Ordinary Joe* all take the love of men and women to absurd extremes. These shows exploit both the viewers' and the participant's obsession for "love." However, much of the "love" on television is really just about sex. One major study conducted by the Parents Television Council states that over half (56 percent) of all television programming contains sexual content and over two thirds of all prime-time shows focus on sex. Some genres of television are nearly completely sex-centered. Soap operas, television movies, and talk shows focus on sex more than 75 percent of the time (see appendix C, Parents Television Council web site). And even though most of the sexual content of these shows is talk as opposed to graphic depictions of sexual behavior, the sexual messages of television do not usually distinguish between marital and extra-marital sex and rarely, if ever, is the morality of sexual behavior discussed. Everybody is just "doing it."

The love of money and things drives the plots of most of the crime shows where people are shown doing almost anything to get the gold. Even kids' cartoons begin the educational process of teaching the love of money by the quest for the pirate's treasure or a desire for all the gold of Fort Knox as a driving force behind the action. Characters are shown clutching, embracing, and lavishing affection on gold coins and paper money as if it were human.

But perhaps the most intense action centers around the love of power—the quest to control the world and the desire to have it all, including the power to determine the destiny of others. This love of power may be the most common plot of all television programs. Stories are written around a premise that getting and keeping power is the greatest love of all. Characters are often motivated by a love of position, a desire for power to control the world, or a need for power to attain what they want. Loving the world and the things of the world is the love theme of television.

GOD'S LOVE IS DIFFERENT

The love of God in the Bible is a love that never seeks its own good but is focused on the other person. It is a love that always hopes for the best in others without seeking something in return and always seeks to benefit the person loved. Although we use the same word, this is not the love of passion for the sake of physical gratification. This is not the love that drives football teammates to stick together to achieve a victory that everyone celebrates. This is not even the intense love of a mother, who would sacrifice all for the child she has borne and sees as part of her very being. God's perfect love covers all this but much more. God's love results in our salvation.

"Love is patient and kind. Love is not jealous or boastful or proud or rude. Love does not demand its own way. Love is not irritable, and it keeps no record of when it has been wronged. It is never glad about injustice but rejoices whenever the truth wins out. Love never gives up, never loses faith, is always hopeful, and endures through every circumstance. Love will last forever" (1 Corinthians 13:4-8, NLT).

TELEVISION REINFORCES THE CONCEPT OF WORKS-BASED RIGHTEOUSNESS

When asked if they are sure they will go to heaven, many people respond with uncertainty. They simply do not know for sure. Often, they will state that they hope that the good things they have done are enough to "get them in." Television programming has played a major part in spreading this false theology of good works or deeds as the price of admission to eternal life with God. Children's cartoons depict characters making choices while miniature angels and devils are perched on their shoulders giving advice and offering eternal choices. The concept of Santa Claus rewarding "good" children with toys and "bad" children with sticks and ashes is woven throughout Christmas programming and commercials. The inherent fairness of good deeds yielding rewards always makes for an appealing story. But this is not biblical nor is it God's plan. God's love makes salvation available to all, regardless of their bad acts or sinful conditions.

Although much of television preaching is about sin and bad behavior and many programs center around justice being served, God has already paid the penalty for the sins of mankind. The love of God allows us to be reconciled with

God through the perfect, sinless sacrifice that was given when Jesus the Christ, God Himself in human form, was crucified. His death was payment for the sins and wrongdoings of everyone. In order to experience this free salvation offered by God, each person must acknowledge that he or she is a sinner and recognize that there is no innocence before God. You simply cannot be good enough. And because of God's love, you don't have to be good enough because He has already provided a substitute for you. You simply have to accept it.

Accepting what God did for you means believing that Jesus did in fact rise from the dead and that the risen Jesus is Lord of your life (Romans 10:9-10). Few people argue about the fact that Jesus was born and lived on earth; however, the Resurrection and the empty tomb are too much for some to consider. But belief in the Resurrection is an integral part of salvation without which all preaching and faith are useless (1 Corinthians 15:14-19). To make Jesus Lord of your life means that you have given Him authority over every aspect of your life here on earth and into the next life. Jesus has assumed responsibility for your past wrongs, so the guilt over those things is covered. Through the Holy Spirit, you are also empowered to resist doing the wrong things that you encounter in the future. But when you do commit a sin, He is now ready to forgive you because you are a part of God's family and have accepted the love of God through faith in Jesus and His sacrifice for you (1 John 1:9).

WHAT YOU NEED TO CONSIDER

God's love expressed through His people leads to salvation. God's people are the way that the message of the

Gospel is to be delivered. It is a message of God's love, not His judgment. As believers share this message with others, God's love is extended through people around the world.

Television programs that reduce Christianity to heaven or hell based on good works corrupt the message of Christianity and the significance of Jesus' sacrifice on the Cross. Recognizing plots and programs that take this approach and being certain to distinguish them, especially for children in your family, is a critical discipline to ensure there is no confusion about the basis of salvation.

God is love and wants all to come to salvation (2 Peter 3:9). While the rejection of God leads to sure damnation and judgment, it is rare that the approach of scaring people into heaven by reminders of the wrath of God will lead to repentance and salvation. It is the good news of the love of God that usually leads to repentance and salvation.

CHAPTER FIVE

TELEVISION– Christianity and Food

THE PROPHET ELIJAH

The Bible introduces us to the prophet Elijah in 1 Kings 17 with the account of Elijah's prophetic announcement of a coming drought to the reigning king, Ahab. Elijah is then instructed by God to go into the wilderness to live by a brook called Cherith, where ravens bring him food during the drought. Though we are not told where Elijah came from or anything about his background, the story makes it clear that he heard from God, that he obeyed God, and that his prophetic voice was authentic and truthful because the drought he prophesied actually came to pass.

Elijah's story also shows that God can and will take supernatural care of his servants, even in the most adverse circumstances. And when circumstances change, as they did in Elijah's story, God can change the plan for survival. Elijah is led away from the brook, and instead of using animals and nature, the survival strategy was changed to a plan that involved using people to support his ministry. A poor widow has been told by God to take care of Elijah. At first, she objects because she is down to her last resources. In the end, she takes Elijah in and they survive the drought through God's miraculous provision of food.

This is the prelude to the incredible story of the ministry of Elijah that continues until 2 Kings 2, when he is taken to heaven by a chariot of fire. Throughout Elijah's ministry, God tells him where to go, what to do and say, and provides food and rest to sustain him through the battles and confrontations with evil and idolatry. This provision is for a purpose to serve humankind and to serve God—and it remains the model for what God continues to do for those He calls and uses in the world today. God calls people and prophets, God provides for them, and God prepares them to serve and stand for the cause of right living and right attitudes toward God and His people. And God pays for what He orders; He provides for those who walk in obedience.

PREACHERS, PROPHETS, AND FOOD

Feeding preachers, especially in the African American tradition, has a long history. After slavery ended in 1865, when thousands of churches were started across the South and the rest of the nation, a good meal was often the only pay a pastor received. Unlike with Elijah, the bird *was the meal* not the bringer of the meal, and most of the time it was probably fried chicken, not raven. The provision for the preacher was God's business and He still uses people to take care of His prophets.

New Testament texts make it clear that God intends for

preachers to be provided for adequately. The admonition to take care of the preachers and elders of the church is clearly laid out, including the need to take extra special care of those who do a good job (1 Corinthians 9:3-14; 1 Timothy 5:17-18). The many roles that local pastors fulfill do more than establish the basis for their compensation. Pastors today serve multiple roles including counselor, financial advisor, teacher, marriage and family therapist, community activist, and many more. In the African American community, where there are often models of ministry that include significant social justice initiatives such as food pantries, clothing banks, and other outreach initiatives, a pastor's responsibilities can sometimes be likened to that of a CEO of a corporation or a high government official with many divisions and subordinates to manage.

However, in each instance, the purpose of the pay is to compensate the service of the preacher, not to provide a reward of "large living" because of some special favor that the people are supposed to endow on God's servant. As in the case of Elijah, the point of provision is rest and preparation for spiritual warfare. This issue of provision for pastors has been often confused as some pastors seek to find their reward in the people's provision, while some people seek to pay their pastor a huge salary so that they may enjoy the vicarious satisfaction of his wealth or material possessions.

Bragging about a pastor's big car or expensive vacation is a poor substitute for having one yourself, but this can become the reason that some people give money to their pastor. They may think, "I can't have it for myself, but my pastor has a Lexus and his wife has one too!" Unfortunately, there are many examples where it appears that this is the reason for the pastor's pay. Jesus said to feed His sheep, not fleece His sheep. Combined with the commercialized culture of acquisition that is driven by our television-saturated society, provision for pastors as God intended it for service and spiritual warfare could be seriously corrupted. But food alone is not enough for pastoral provision and God has a greater plan.

FINDING GOD IN THE FOOD BUSINESS

According to 2003 estimates of the National Chicken Council, chicken generates over $30 billion a year in sales revenue (see appendix C, National Chicken Council web site). Chicken, often associated with good preaching and fed to pastors at home and in restaurants, is big business. The food industry is so big today that we have the Food Network on television, along with dozens of cooking shows. Food Network president, Judy Girard, was quoted as saying, "The family that cooks together stays together" (Richmond 2003, S-4), suggesting perhaps that food and television could do more for families than prayer! But the Food Network does not exist to keep families together. They want their share of the over $5 billion that is spent each year on food advertising. At this point in history you would think with all this advertising and emphasis on food, that the problem of making sure that everyone in the world has enough food to eat would be solved by now, but it isn't.

According to the U.S. Department of Agriculture, in 2002 over 3.8 million families reached the point where someone skipped a meal because they could not afford one. In addition, 12 million families lacked money for food and 32 percent actually experienced hunger at one time or another

(Nord, 2003). This sad state of affairs exists in the country that could feed the world with its food production. We have the resources, infrastructure, and economic incentive to do it; but without leadership and the will to take on the challenge of world hunger, the U.S. remains disobedient to the moral and ethical responsibility to address the most basic of human needs—hunger.

And this is not simply the political problem of the federal government taking on goals like space exploration instead of solving hunger. In most local communities, the opportunity to make a difference in the life of a hungry family or hungry and homeless individual is nearby. Enough food is wasted to support entire ministries like America's Second Harvest and others who seek to pass on food that would otherwise be thrown away.

Poor eating habits are the other side of the food problem. Most television advertising is for processed foods, snack foods, and junk foods. Image and lifestyle advertising is used strategically to convince you to buy foods that have limited nutritional value and create health problems from imbalanced diets (see appendix D). The result is that much of the U.S. population is overweight, while at that same time we have a hunger problem, says Neville Rigby in a *USA Today* article (A. 14). This is a particularly bad problem in the African American community. Its roots lie in poor dietary practices that began in slavery and have continued as a result of economic disparities and lack of access to quality foods in many African American neighborhoods. Add to this the dietary problems caused by all the excess calories in the 40 ounce malt liquor bottles. The cost of not taking care of the "temple" is early death. According to the USDA, diseases and conditions such as coronary heart disease, cancer, stroke, diabetes, and hypertension all have some connection to poor eating habits and cause half of all deaths (Frazao 1999, 5-6).

WHAT YOU NEED TO CONSIDER

Physical inactivity directly results in obesity and weight gain, and television watching is one of the most passive activities we do. A gain of 11-18 pounds doubles the risk of developing Type 2 diabetes, while weight loss reduces that risk. Children are particularly at risk as poor eating habits and lack of physical activity become lifestyle practices that continue into adulthood and result in disease and obesity. A study done in New York found that only 29% of African Americans are meeting recommended levels of physical activity (see appendix E).

Watching less television and becoming physically active reduces the exposure to advertising that encourages poor eating habits and directly addresses a major risk factor for illness and disease. The Center for Disease Control has calculated that inactive adults spend $330 more per year in direct medical costs than active adults; so watching television less often could actually save you money. This savings is multiplied when you include the reduction of impulse and fast food purchases that results from avoiding commercials.

Fasting is a biblical discipline, which when combined with prayer can produce life-changing results. One food relief ministry, World Vision, has a national program of fasting to increase awareness of world hunger (see appendix C, World Vision web site). The idea is to get others to understand and experience what it feels like to be hungry and to become motivated to address the problem through support of their global hunger initiatives. Many ministries operate food banks and support local hunger initiatives only as a once a year Thanksgiving activity. However, hunger is an everyday occurrence. Is it possible that God wants you or your ministry to engage in an ongoing feeding program that can wipe out hunger in your community?

Church activities centered on food should support the changed diet and health-related issues that dramatically affect our nation and African Americans in particular. The traditional after-church service dinners and weekend food sales can be just as appealing and enjoyable with healthy foods as they are with the high fat, low nutritional value options, which people have become used to. Some churches have changed the ingredients of some dishes to offer healthier alternatives such as using turkey instead of salt pork for seasoning or adding more fresh fruits and vegetables to the menus. It is also a good idea to have health-related events as often as food-related events. Blood pressure screenings and health fairs are easy to implement since most churches have health care workers who are part of the membership.

Donating food, money, or both should be a part of every ministry and every Christian's ministry efforts. World hunger is a problem that can be solved. Taking dominion in this area of activity is one where immediate victories are possible and of which life and health can result for those in need. God is our Provider, but He also wants to use us to bring provision to others.

CHAPTER SIX

TELEVISION— Violence and God's Protection

JACOB EXPERIENCES GOD'S PROTECTION

In Genesis 25, we read that Jacob was on the run. He had conspired with his mother to trick his father into giving him a blessing that should have gone to his older brother Esau. His brother found out and vowed to kill him. Esau was a hunter and was very good with weapons; therefore, this was no idle threat—he was probably very serious about it. The fact was that this was not the first time Esau had been ripped off by his brother. Jacob had taken advantage of Esau's hunger after a long hunting trip and convinced Esau to give him his birthright in exchange for food. The birthright was a special honor that allowed firstborn sons to receive a double portion of the family inheritance along with the leadership rights to the family, but it could be sold or given away.

As if that wasn't bad enough, the local girls who were interested in marrying Jacob were probably tempting him. His family had money and he was a good catch but his mother had no interest in Jacob having a cross-cultural marriage like his brother Esau (Genesis 25:5, 11; 27:46) whose wives were already causing problems (Genesis 26:34-35). The solution to both of these problems was for Jacob to leave and do it quickly. His mother, who had caused much of this problem in the first place, arranged for him to go to a relative's place over 200 miles away (Genesis 27:42-45). In the midst of his fear-filled fugitive's journey, Jacob has an encounter with God that changes his life forever (Genesis 28:10-21). With certain death at his heels, Jacob strikes a deal with God that even the television actor from the *Fugitive* may not have done.

IS DEATH THE WORST THING THAT CAN HAPPEN TO YOU?

According to Jesus, death is not the worst thing that can happen. Jesus said that we should not be afraid of people who can only kill the body, but rather we should fear the one who can destroy both the body and the soul—that is God (Matthew 10:28). But if you consider Jacob's experience with fear and running, his reaction was pretty typical. He was running for his life. We don't like to talk about it, but the truth is, despite all the preaching and talking about heaven, few people really want to go. We would just as soon wait until "our time is up," or some other excuse. Every now and then you will meet some person (usually older) who can sincerely express the sentiment shared by Paul when he said, "For I am now ready to be offered, and the time of my departure is at hand. I have fought a good fight, I have finished my course" (2 Timothy 4:6-7, KJV). But for most, the view is usually, "I want to go to heaven; just not now."

Yet we know that there is life beyond the physical. Whether we arrive at this knowledge through an experience like the one Jacob had, the birth of a child, a near death experience, or some other way, approaching death and its transformation without fear is one of the great teachings of the Bible. Paul's admonition to the Thessalonians that we should not be as those who have no hope in life after death, is more important than ever today (1 Thessalonians 4:13). The widespread fear that has been thrust upon the nation and the world by those who do not fear death—the terrorists and suicide bombers—can only be quenched by faith in these teachings. In a battle against an adversary that does not fear death, you cannot win if you do fear death. It is even worse when the adversary believes that death is a good thing because his current life is so miserable. This is the situation we face today in so many places around the world.

TELEVISION TEACHES FEAR OF DEATH

Television has raised the fear of death to new and higher levels than ever by taking death and violence as entertainment to extremes that would have been unthinkable even a few years ago. Death has been defined as the most important topic of television news. The more the story involves death, the more the important the story. The more gruesome the death, the higher the level of coverage. The greater the death toll, the more times the story will be repeated. The saying in the newsroom is "if it bleeds, it leads" the nightly newscast.

War reporting has been turned into a type of reality TV miniseries. Each network gives their coverage of war a television program type name, blurring the lines between what is real and what is entertainment. Embedding reporters in military units for "live action" coverage further pushes the limits of war as televised entertainment and offers the possibility of live action, and on-screen images of death. All this raises the fear of death even more and makes us ever more vulnerable to the threats and actions of those who do not fear death.

TELEVISION AND VIOLENCE

Television's obsession with violence is just as intense and frequent as the deaths it often leads to. In addition to raising our fears, violent acts on television have many consequences. Violence on television desensitizes us to violence in daily life. Violence is taught as an acceptable way of solving problems. Children, criminals, and even otherwise reasonable adults imitate violence on television as constant viewing transforms people's values and shapes behavior.

Social scientists have conducted hundreds of studies linking violence on television to violent behavior, especially in children. Many others have conducted studies that aim to show there is no connection. A University of Michigan study concludes, "the relationship between TV violence viewing and aggression in childhood has been...demonstrated [and] childhood exposure to media violence predicts young adult aggressive behavior for both males and females" (Huesmann 2003, 203).

While there may be room for debate about some of the studies, few would conclude that the ever-increasing violence on television is a good thing. A study conducted by The Parents Television Council (PTC) showed that in the five-year period from 1998-2002, the total number of depictions of violent acts increased 41 percent during the family viewing hours of 8:00 p.m. and increased 134 percent during the 9:00 p.m. hour. UPN, ABC, and Fox had the highest rates of violence in this study (see appendix F).

WHAT YOU NEED TO CONSIDER

Watching less television means seeing less violence. Given the above statistics, if your time spent watching television was cut in half from four hours a day to two hours a day, you would still be seeing the same amount of violence. That shows just how much more violence is now on television these days. The American Academy of Child and Adolescent Psychiatry (AACAP) has concluded that children who watch a lot of television are likely to (see appendix C, AACAP web site):

- have lower grades in school
- read fewer books
- exercise less
- be overweight

We can add that these children and adults are also more likely to be fearful and to develop a view of death as the worst thing that can happen to them. Turning the television off is a good starting point to avoid these negative effects. Substituting other activities will help complete the lifestyle transition that would be more consistent with keeping the spotlight on Jesus and away from the violence of television.

Video games use the television as a device to give you hands-on experience with fear, violence, and death. One of the top selling video games of 2003, "Grand Theft Auto: ViceCity" has a sequence that allows players to pick up prostitutes and beat them to death, complete with sound effects for further enhancement. Allowing children to play these games is irresponsible. Not knowing that they were this bad may have been understandable before you read this, but now you know. Get rid of it. It should be noted that the ratings on these games, like the ratings on movies, often understate the extent of violence and sexually explicit content. You have to check them out. Video game content should be very carefully evaluated as many churches consider making their youth ministries more "cutting edge" by introducing video games and other "innovative" approaches to keep youth in church.

Funeral services need to be home going celebrations. The celebratory funeral is a tradition in many African cultures where there is clear acceptance of the fact of the afterlife and the transitional nature of all life. Rejoicing in the contributions of a person's life and focusing on the fact that "this world is not our home [and] we are looking forward to our city in heaven, which is yet to come" (Hebrews 13:14, NLT), reminds us not to cling to this life as if there is nothing else. Movies and television shows on death and horror should not be entertainment for those who understand that death is not the end. Let this truth change the funerals of believers from despair-driven, hopeless happenings to celebrations of life.

Talking about television violence and doing something about it are two different things. A number of groups are actively engaged in trying to change what we see on television. There is a broad range of groups and many different agendas, but all seek to reduce the violence and killing and make television more family friendly. Organizations like LimiTV, Inc. and TV Turnoff are definitely places for you or your church to get involved in reducing the amount of violence our children see on television (see appendix C, LimiTV, Inc. and TV Turnoff web sites).

CHAPTER SEVEN

TELEVISION— Hip-Hop and Sin

JESUS DIED FOR YOUR SINS

While it is true that God could have come to earth under whatever conditions in whatever form and for whatever reason He wanted to, the reason He actually came was to deal with murder, rape, adultery, treachery, gossip, lying, and the rest. You know, those things we have become so immune to because we view it every day and have allowed our hearts to become hardened to its impact. John the Baptist introduced Jesus that way in John 1:29 (NLT), with the announcement, "Look! There is the Lamb of God who takes away the sin of the world!" and Jesus Himself plainly said, "my blood seals the covenant between God and his people. It is poured out to forgive the sins of many" (Matthew 26:28, NLT). Many references in Scripture point out this central purpose in Christ's coming—to die for our sins (1 Corinthians 15:3; 1 Timothy 1:15; 1 John 1:7b).

As A.P. Gibbs stated in the book entitled *Worship: The Christians' Highest Occupation,* "There can be no approach to God, no standing before God, no acceptance with God, no pardon from God, and no worship to God, apart from an acceptable substitutionary sacrifice which bears the sinner's sins, takes his place, died in his stead and is accepted by God on his behalf" (178).

The difficulty many of us have with this fact of Scripture rests in the conviction that we are better than most people and therefore not worthy of the judgment that the Bible says that we are all under. More significantly, we lack appreciation of the true holiness of God. When you understand the holiness of God, you understand the worthlessness of sacrifices of praise, good works, or any other effort that we offer from our own righteousness as acceptable for God. God is simply too good for you, and the standard of perfection set by the life He lived as Christ makes all other efforts futile.

Jesus paid the penalty of sin by submitting to one of the most brutal forms of execution ever. Crucifixion had been practiced many years before the execution of Christ, though we commonly associate it with Him alone. The slow death of asphyxiation and blood loss that resulted from being nailed to a cross you had to carry to your own place of death was probably as bloody and demeaning as the recent film, *The Passion of the Christ,* depicted it to be. It is hard to accept that this type of death had to be experienced for the things we may have done wrong. Most of us do not feel we have done anything at all to deserve death, much less a crucifixion. But the Bible has declared us all guilty before God.

By creating categories of sin that make certain sins worse than others, we have learned to excuse ourselves and others.

Many actually feel confident that their lives are perfect before God, based on certain behaviors or practices that they faithfully adhere to. Watching episodes of *Jerry Springer*, where mother and daughter are sharing the same date, can make your gossiping or lying seem like a small thing. Jesus addressed this issue as well by reminding us that God's standard of righteousness extends even to the thought life, a place where all of us can be found guilty of negative thinking nearly every day (Psalm 94:11; 139:23-24). Much of this can be traced in part to television's treatment of sin and our constant exposure to it.

TELEVISION PROMOTES SIN

Television provides a very accurate historical record of the decline of values in society to moral relativism. When you examine television programming by decade from the 1950s forward, the period during which a majority of Americans first had television in their homes, you see a decade by decade transformation of values from a biblical worldview to the current situation that is more like that described in the book of Judges, where it was said, "every man did that which was right in his own eyes" (Judges 21:25, KJV).

This transformation, from married couples sleeping in separate twin beds in the situation comedies of the 1950s and 1960s to the current blatant promiscuity of programs like *Sex in the City*, indicates something has definitely happened. Whether television is leading or following is an argument for the sociologists, but television is certainly broadcasting a different message today than it was 20 or even 10 years ago. We all know this, and most people will say they do not like it, yet we watch it anyway. We participate in the promotion of sinful lifestyles and behavior on television; and though we talk about it, few are moved to take action.

TELEVISION, HIP-HOP, AND AMERICAN CULTURE

One of the most phenomenal transformations of culture has been the emergence of the hip-hop movement from the African American community into the mainstream through television exposure. The Black Entertainment Television Network (BET), which began as a programming alternative to serve the entire Black population, was soon reduced to a wasteland of informercials and free music videos provided by record companies trying to sell music. Hip-Hop music videos quickly devolved into a downward spiral of misogynistic (woman-hating) lyrics, depictions of promiscuous sexuality, and violence. Despite many well-meaning social critics' attempts to legitimize these videos and CDs as nothing more than the latest version of counter-culture postmodern artistic expression "keeping it real by keeping it raunchy," the reality is that their existence owes much more to the market capitalism and the media oligopoly than anything else. Some of the same companies that bring you television sell most of these CDs.

The invention of White rapper Eminem and the continued penetration of hip-hop into White culture have made the non-African American sales of this music genre the most important part. Just as Elvis Presley transformed African American rock and roll music into an expression that White American teens could easily digest, hip-hop has given the White teen audience a virtual cafeteria of sensate debauchery that seems to have something negative for everyone. This is clearly not the first time the image of the Black man as a criminal or thug has been elevated by the media (perhaps the late Ron O' Neal's movie *Superfly* deserves that honor), but it is certainly the deepest penetration of negative Black images as cultural icons imitated by White youth, even worldwide.

The good news is that despite the nearly overwhelmingly negative images of Black teens on television, the reality is that the majority of African American teens are God-fearing, church-attending, family-centered kids, who have positive outlooks on life. The Centers for Disease Control reports that African American teens have lower involvement than Whites in virtually all the high-risk behaviors including drug use, smoking, and alcohol abuse. Though there are no definitive studies that document the reason for this, one could speculate that the higher church attendance of African American adults and teens could account for these differences. The irony is that African American teens exhibit better behaviors despite watching significantly more television than Whites.

WHAT YOU NEED TO CONSIDER

"I will set nothing wicked before my eyes" (Psalm 101:3) is a promise that many Christians need to make regarding viewing choices on television. Guarding our minds and our thoughts against sin and violence by watching television less often should be the first approach to the problem. After all, if the researchers are right that violence on television causes violent behavior (and sin on television causes sinful behavior), why risk it? Especially with your children. If the researchers are wrong, you have obeyed the admonition of Scripture and you are still better off than if you watched it.

The best way to counter negative hip-hop is to promote

holy hip-hop. There is no getting around the fact that young people want counter-cultural social icons. A large but under-promoted and under-distributed group of artists and ministers are promoting the message of Jesus Christ in the hip-hop genre. Recognizing that there is a difference and supporting those who have a biblical message and worldview, though it may be presented in an unfamiliar format, is a response that you and your church should consider. The message is more important than the method.

Desensitization occurs when we continuously view negative images. What was once shocking is no longer unusual when it is seen over and over again. The first time you watch an episode of the *Sopranos*, replete with violent acts and laced with foul language, it takes you off guard. By the time you have watched enough episodes to know the characters, you actually expect them to curse or do something violent. You have become desensitized, and you have accepted this behavior as the norm. What have you opened yourself up to that used to bother you? How have you changed as a result?

CHAPTER EIGHT

TELEVISION—
Life After Death

TELEVISION AND LIFE AFTER DEATH

What sets Christianity apart from all other religious faiths is the fact of the Resurrection. Jesus' final proof that He was who He said He was, was presented in His bodily comeback from death. The 40-day period of Jesus' appearances after His crucifixion included encounters with His disciples and many others. We cannot know why He did not stay even longer, but we do understand that for those who saw Him, touched Him, and shared meals with Him after the Resurrection, the impact was life transforming. Jesus told them that they believed because they saw Him, but that those who have believed *without* seeing Him are blessed (John 20:29).

It is easy to consider the impact of this event in the context of the times. Never before, or since, had the public death of a spiritual leader been followed by His return to life. With

Jesus' numerous appearances, shock and awe overtook the world so that to this day, the faith continues. These were not times of fictional literature or television specials. These reports came from eyewitness encounters of people who had seen something that changed their very lives—the living Christ. No other spiritual leader had done it before and none has since. Muhammad, Buddha, and all others lie dead in their graves. But the grave could not hold Jesus and there is no body today; the tomb is empty.

FAITH IN CHRIST IS FAITH IN THE RESURRECTION

More than anything else, believing in Christ is believing in His bodily resurrection and the proof of His deity that rests in this occurrence. After His resurrection, Jesus had to show the disciples the severe damage to His hands and His side from the crucifixion and challenge Thomas to actually touch Him before he would believe. Once the issue of His resurrection had been resolved, Jesus was able to give His followers commands to evangelize and make disciples. Their fears were transformed to an empowered witness because they knew for certain that Jesus was able to overcome death and the natural order to accomplish His purposes.

LIFE AFTER DEATH—THE TELEVISION VERSION

The television version of life after death is a fear-filled experience. This is not supposed to happen. The reactions are either comedy or horror, ranging from *The Addams Family* and *Dark Shadows* to *Buffy, the Vampire Slayer* and *The X Files*. When the dead are depicted walking around on television, it is a real problem. The weight of these images rests in the understanding that these things are not supposed to happen.

Yet, this is exactly what Christianity teaches did happen in the case of Christ. You must believe in the Resurrection or you do not believe in the living Christ.

The constant reinforcement of afterlife encounters in television programming as either comedy or horror has the effect of teaching people not to take the Resurrection seriously and to diminish the reality of the spiritual or the demonic. The recent fascination with angels presents a clear contrast to what has been a long line of television images of the afterlife as extremely spooky and fearful. The Scripture is very clear that the realm of the Spirit is very real and the presence of life absent from a body is a fact.

AFRICAN CULTURE AND AFTERLIFE

In the African cultural tradition, the afterlife seems to be a widely-accepted reality. Paying tribute to ancestors is done with an understanding that their passage from this life was not a passage *from* existence, but a passage *to* an existence outside of the physical world we share. Negative spiritual associations with voodoo, root working, and other occult beliefs and practices survived slavery and often have a presence in the Black community even today. We know from Scripture that there are those whose practice of the occult arts are directly linked to the demonic forces that are in the world (Acts 19:13-19). Television has ridiculed and reduced these practices to the things of witch doctors and ignorant tribal belief systems. But at a minimum, they affirm the deep cultural traditions of a worldview that includes life in the spirit.

WHAT YOU NEED TO CONSIDER

Focusing on the resurrected Christ keeps the reality of the living Christian faith as a part of the daily experience. When we believe that Christ rose and lives today, our prayer is empowered, our faith is strengthened, and our behavior changes. The dead are history, the living shape history, and Christ is among the living.

Elevation of Resurrection Day, or Easter, to its proper place of prominence brings the church in line with the major distinction of the Christian faith. We serve a risen Savior, He is in the world today, and He lives. Always have an Easter program and work hard to assure that the Resurrection gets as much emphasis as Christmas.

Hell is real. You do not die and just float around in some ghostly purgatory as depicted in some television scenes. The existence of a literal hell, a place of damnation and punishment, is not as widely held today, in part because so many television shows portray people dying and going to the "light" or some other non-negative experience. This is not the teaching of the Bible.

CHAPTER NINE

TELEVISION—God's People At Worship

CAN YOU WORSHIP AT A TELEVISION CHURCH?

Worship is our response to the perception of the presence of God. You worship when you ascribe "worth" to something, worth above and beyond anything else present. Praise is related since praise involves speaking highly of someone or something, but praise has its limits. We praise our children or our employees when they do a good job; but we do not worship them ever, or at least we should not. Psalm 95 illustrates this connection perfectly. The psalmist begins with a call to sing and cry out to God because of His greatness but then begins to talk about (praise) the "good job" God did in making the earth. After considering all His creative majesty, the only response possible is worship because God's creation gives evidence that His worth is above all else present. He is the Lord our Maker.

Praise has taken the psalmist to a place where he worships God (Kenoly 1996, 81-84).

Psalm 100 similarly begins in praise and ends in worship. The more you talk about or sing about the goodness of God and the joy that is ours because we know that He is, the sooner your praise will become worship. Our worship can be intelligent and sincere because our knowledge of who He is comes from the Scriptures. Our understanding of His greatness rests in our belief of the testimonies of the text. The more Scripture you know, the more praise will flow from your heart and mouth as you recognize that God is worthy of worship.

JESUS AND WORSHIP

In His conversation at the well with the woman in John 4, Jesus shares that true worshipers worship in spirit and in truth and directly addresses the issue of the importance or rather the non-importance of the place of worship. The woman changes the subject to worship after Jesus demonstrates His deity by telling her the story of her life. When you encounter the presence of God, that awareness results in worship. In verse 20 of the text, the woman then raises the matter of whether the mountain or Jerusalem is the right place to worship, which leads to Jesus' response that neither is the right place.

Jesus' concern is with the spiritual condition of the worshiper and the relationship of the worshiper with God, the focus of our worship. This is far more important than whether the worship is at a church building, in a crowd, at home alone, or even alone in front of a television. The sincerity of the worshiper and the spirit-led prompting to worship are the main issues, not the location.

Dr. Vashti McKenzie states the critical connection then between worship and hearing from God apart from the matter of location: "We worship God in spirit and in truth, both corporately, with others, and privately, alone. It is a refreshing experience anytime, anywhere, for anyone on the path to personal revelation. The public and private worship of God, including prayer, fasting, praise, and sabbaticals is a powerful place from which to hear God. We must listen for God through worship, not only listen to the TV for salvation" (202).

ALONE WITH GOD AND MY TELEVISION

Despite the clarity around this point that location and numbers of people do not define worship, Scripture is also very clear that fellowship, or the sharing of companionship with others of similar beliefs, is important to God. Acts 2:44-47 describes the church as "believers gathered together," "meeting together," "eating together," and "praising God" together in the temple courts. The writer of Hebrews 10:25 encourages believers not to give up meeting together. Jesus also suggests that His presence manifests in the gathering of believers (Matthew 18:20).

So while it may be true that the Bible does not forbid or condemn worship alone or with your favorite church program on television, this cannot be a substitute for the clear instructions and directions from God concerning the coming together of believers. The many instructions to believers to love (John 13:34), forgive (Luke 6:37), encourage (1 Thessalonians 4:18), and pray (James 5:16) for one another are not really possible apart from gathering and fellowship with other believers. "Bedside Baptist" and "Television Tabernacle" can never be substitutes for the gathering together with other believers that is seen in the New Testament church of Acts 4.

WORSHIP AND GIVING

We first encounter the word *worship* in the Bible when Abraham has been asked by God to go to the mountain to sacrifice his son Isaac. Abraham describes this offering of a sacrifice to his servants in Genesis 22:5 as "worship." Giving up something that is precious, whether it is the sacrifice of personal pride through uplifted hands to God or the giving of monetary gifts to help those less fortunate and fund the work of the church, is a form of worship. Worship always involves sacrifice.

Supporting ministries that are televised or supporting your own church's television ministry through giving brings an element of sacrifice to the worship experience. Some suggest that supporting national ministries that are televised is at odds with support of the local church. It may be considered that giving should no more be limited to a specific place than worship should be confined to a place. But like the concept of collective worship, it is hard to imagine that giving to television ministries only is an appropriate substitute for the type of collective giving to the local church that we see in Acts 2. This giving should be "in addition to" so that like all worship and giving, the more you give, the more God is honored.

WHAT YOU NEED TO CONSIDER

Worshiping alone with television or corporately at a church is a less important issue than worshiping in spirit and in truth. What matters most to God is the heart of the worshiper, not the place of the worship. If you have come to a place where your worship is sincere, this is more critical to God than the place where you reached that sincerity. The woman at the well in John 4 was at a place of deep disconnectedness from her community when she encountered Jesus, but her testimony transformed a community because of the sincerity of her encounter.

Involvement in church worship is a command in Scripture, not an option that can be substituted with television time. The answer to the question of whether the right, best, or the more acceptable way to worship is alone at home or together in church is simply that God wants both; corporate and private worship are both necessary for the maturity of the believer and the honor of God. If you only worship alone, you have not obeyed Hebrews 10:25. If you always need others around you to worship, then you may not have truly had the experience of being alone with God and sincerely experiencing His presence.

Giving is worship, and worship always involves sacrifice. There is no limit to giving, which means that you could give in worship to television ministries or to your local church and be a blessing to God and others. However, there is a greater accountability to the giver when you are giving in the local church and have the ability through reports and church meetings to know that the contributions reached their intended purpose. Many legitimate-sounding charities and ministries using television solicitation have turned out to be engaged in fraudulent practices, so it is important to do some investigation before you decide to let a television program direct your giving (see appendix G).

We do seem to worship everything else but the Lord. The Oscars, the Emmys, the Grammys, the lifestyles of the rich, the exploits of the athletes, and the many, many celebrities who we imitate in dress, speech, and even in the way we do our hair indicate that we ascribe "worth" to people and things other than the living God. God requires our worship of Him and Him alone.

CHAPTER TEN

TELEVISION–The World of Reality

CHRISTIAN LIVING IN A WORLD OF REALITY TELEVISION

A winner of a reality television show was being interviewed and asked about what she was doing with the money she had won. She told of real estate investments and other investing activities and described a life that seemed to be focused on keeping the earnings she had won and making the best return on her winnings. A long struggle including personal exposure and humiliation in front of millions of television viewers had been the price for this prize, and she intended to make the most of it for herself and her family. Once again, the message that money is the main thing, no matter what it takes to get it, is presented by television as the goal of life.

PUTTING YOUR MONEY WHERE YOUR FAITH IS

Joseph, a successful real estate investor, sells his land and gives the total proceeds to the fledgling Christian movement led by Peter and John. They use the funds to help those who are in need, providing a church-based welfare system to assist those followers who are less fortunate. They also support the ministry of healing and teaching the people about the resurrected Christ with the funds provided by the land sale. Their influence on Joseph leads him to make a commitment to full-time ministry. He is nicknamed Barnabas, a name meaning "son of encouragement," lived a life that was focused on helping people, and went out of his way to be kind to others and to make provision for those who were poor and needy (Acts 4:36-37).

One of the most critical roles that Barnabas played in the development of the early church involved his encouragement of Paul and later, Mark. Local Christians did not trust Paul because he had been such an enemy of the early church before his conversion. They thought Paul's story might have been simply a trick to capture and kill more Christians who were under persecution at that time. Risking his life, Barnabas reached out to Paul, met with him, and then convinced others that Paul's conversion was sincere. There are often select people whom God uses to encourage those who become great leaders. Barnabas was such a person for Paul (Acts 9:27-15:39).

Barnabas also encouraged Mark to go with him and Paul to Antioch. During this first missionary journey, Mark left and returned home, thereby disappointing Paul (Acts 13:13). But Barnabas remained open to inviting Mark on another trip even though Paul disagreed. Barnabas separated from Paul to include Mark in his missionary efforts (Acts 15:36-39). This encouragement of Mark proved to be worthwhile as Mark turned out to have an effective ministry and joined Paul later in other missions work (2 Timothy 4:11). It is this kind of encouragement and results that causes Barnabas to be described as "a good man, full of the Holy Spirit and strong in faith" (Acts 11:24, NLT).

SPREADING THE GOSPEL TO THE TELEVISION GENERATION

Seeing people through God's eyes and always looking for the best requires close fellowship with God that results from prayer, studying God's Word, and determining that the rule of love will guide your decisions. Love always hopes for the best (1 Corinthians 13:7). This can be difficult because so much of the prevailing perspective on the condition of mankind is drawn from the constant negative imagery of the television and films. Young people always seem to be portrayed as selfish, foolish, or rebellious. Older people are frequently shown as worthless or controlling. Women are often manipulative or silly. The men who seem to have good judgment or compassion are White; while non-whites typically play sports and use ungrammatical and ignorant sounding speech (see appendix H).

If we do not constantly guard our thoughts, we may project these images upon those around us and make bad judgments about godly people who look like or remind us of televised images but who, in fact, are far from it. Teens are particularly vulnerable to this type of stereotyping because they all seem to dress like *thugs* today whether they live like them or not. The racial prejudices that can arise from media images prevent African American male corporate executives from catching taxicabs as much as they lead African American youth to assume that their White teacher "has it in for them." Christian discernment leaves the door open for all of us to act as Barnabas did and see those who are willing to be used by God to make a difference in society.

LIVING THE GOSPEL

Knowing the power of television to shape perception, thoughts, and beliefs should lead to changed behavior. The Christian is encouraged to be transformed by the renewing of the mind and to be certain to manage the thought life in such a way that every thought is brought into obedience to Christ (Romans 12:1-2; 2 Corinthians 10:5). This should mean that a casual, uncritical, channel surfing form of television watching is not a part of the life of a disciplined follower of Christ. The risks are too great. This is especially true for children, for whom we have a special obligation to bring up in a way that encourages their faithfulness and obedience to the principles and precepts of the Christian faith. This is our most critical responsibility and is the legacy that will follow us far into the future.

For some, this may mean becoming an activist and a missionary to the television industry itself. While everyone has a stake in making certain that the assault on the woman seen in the 2004 Super Bowl halftime show or the misleading projections about political candidates are not broadcast through our country, some people may have a special calling to fight to change media either from the inside or the outside. Organizations that seek to reform media are listed in appendix C.

PRESERVING THE GOSPEL THROUGH MEDIA

The power of television as a means of transmission of the

Gospel of Jesus Christ has yet to be fully realized if one thinks of the definition of "mass media" in the sense that Marshall McLuhan wrote in the classic work *Understanding Media: The Extension of Man*. McLuhan contends that "mass media is not as much an indication of the size of the audience as it is the fact that everybody becomes involved in them at the same time" (349).

WHAT YOU NEED TO CONSIDER

"Love the Lord your God with all your heart and with all your soul and with all your mind. This is the first and the greatest commandment" (Matthew 22:37b-38, NIV). In order to do this in the world today, you must watch what you watch. You cannot casually allow the television to give you new visions that are not of God as you watch hours and hours each week without spending at least the same or ideally a greater amount of time in prayer and study of the Word of God. God is not looking for a love that includes some of your mind, that part that is left over after your favorite show. God wants all of your mind.

"Love your neighbor as yourself" (Matthew 22:39, NIV). Living out the love of God and transforming the lives of those around us is the great commandment upon which all the Law is founded. If you are constantly feeding your mind the negative and ungodly images and stories from the media content of today and if your mind has been corrupted to the point that you think watching the pain of other people on crude and violent television talk shows is entertainment, you have not been loving yourself very well. Begin to love yourself by first transforming your mind with the Word of God, and then watch as God begins to use you to bring about transformation in the lives of others. You have to decide that you are going to obey the commands of God. You have to decide that you are going to love your neighbor.

Lead others to the truth of the Gospel, "make disciples . . . teach [them] to obey [Jesus' commands]" (Matthew 28:19-20, NLT). Both this great commission and the great commandment above requires that we be self-controlled and alert because our adversary actively seeks to distract us from these purposes. Television has proven its power of distraction. Your personal activities in leading others to truth can be extremely compromised by bondage to the boob tube or your fixation on the flat screen. Your ministry activities and the efforts of your church need to include active efforts to push back on the influence of negative media in your community and in the lives of others. This is your assignment.

Appendixes

Table of Contents

Number of Hours Spent Watching Various Media Types

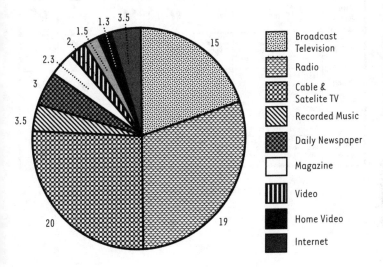

Broadcast Television

Radio

Cable & Satelite TV

Recorded Music

Daily Newspaper

Magazine

Video

Home Video

Internet

Source: Peers, Martin "Buddy, Can You Spare Some Time?" *The Wall Street Journal*, 26 January 2004, B1

APPENDIX B
Major Television Media Companies

	TELEVISION INTEREST	ONLINE	MAGAZINES	THEME PARKS	BOOKS	MUSIC
TIME WARNER	**HBO, The WB,** Cinemax, Court TV, TBS Superstation, Cartoon Network, CNN	✔	✔	✔	✔	✔
DISNEY	**ABC** Television, Disney Channel, Fox Kids, ESPN, Lifetime, A&E,	✔	✔	✔	✔	
VIACOM	**CBS,** MTV, VH1, ShowTime, The Movie Channel, **BET, UPN,** Nickelodeon			✔	✔	✔
NEWS CORP	**FOX** Entertainment Group, Fox Movie Channel, Fox News Channel, FX, National Geographic Channel, Direct TV		✔		✔	
GENERAL ELECTRIC	**NBC,** Paxson, Telemundo, CNBC, MSNBC, History Channel	✔				✔

Source: McChesney, Robert W. Rich Media, Poor Democracy: Communicating Politics in Dubious Times, New York: The New Press, 2000.

APPENDIX C
Websites

www.aacap.org *(American Academy of Child & Adolescent Psychiatry)*

www.abiworld.org *(American Bankruptcy Institute)*

www.commercialalert.org *(Commercial Alert)*

www.federalreserve.gov *(Board of Governors of the Federal Reserve System)*

www.iwantmedia.com *(I Want Media)*

www.limitv.org *(LimiTV, Inc.)*

www.mediachannel.org *(MediaChannel.org)*

www.nationalchickencouncil.com *(National Chicken Council)*

www.nielsen.com *(Nielsen Media Research)*

www.parentstv.org *(Parents Television Council)*

www.pfo.org *(Personal Freedom Outreach)*

www.tvturnoff.org *(TV Turnoff Network)*

www.targetmarketnews.com *(Target Market News)*

www.worldvision.org *(World Vision)*

FOOD ADVERTISING STRATEGIES

Excitement Who could ever have imagined that food could be so much fun? One bite of a snack food and you're surfing in California or soaring on your skateboard!

Star Power Your favorite sports star or celebrity is telling you that their product is the best! Kids listen, without realizing that the star is being paid to promote the product.

Bandwagon Join the crowd! Don't be left out! Everyone is buying the latest snack food. Aren't you?

Scale Advertisers make a product look bigger or smaller than it actually is.

Repetition Advertisers hope that if you see the product or hear its name over and over again, you will be more likely to buy it. Sometimes the same commercial will be repeated over and over again.

Sounds Good Music and other sound effects add to the excitement of commercials, especially commercials aimed at kids. Those little jingles that you just can't get out of your head are another type of music used to make you think of the product. Have you ever noticed that the sound volume of commercials is higher than the program that follows?

Cartoon Characters Tony the Tiger sells cereal and the Nestle's Nesquik Bunny sells chocolate milk. Cartoon characters like these, make kids identify with products.

Omission Advertisers oftentimes don't give you the full story about their products. For example, when a Pop-Tart claims to be "part" of a healthy breakfast, it doesn't mention that the breakfast might still be healthy with or without this product.

Are You Cool Enough? Advertisers may try to convince you that if you don't use their products, you are a nerd. Usually advertisers show people that look uncool trying a product, and then suddenly they become hip-looking and begin doing cool things.

"Food Advertising Strategies" Student Handout. © 2004 Media Awareness Network, www.media-awareness.ca Adapted with permission.

APPENDIX E
Physical Inactivity

Physical Inactivity
Who Is Meeting Recommended Activity Levels?

42% of adults overall
31% of people 65 and over
29% African Americans
32% of people with less than a high school education
39% of people making less than $15,000
28% of people with disabilities

Source: Patricia Hess, Director Division of Nutrition New York State Department of Health

APPENDIX F
VIOLENCE DURING PRIME TIME
BROADCAST TELEVISION

8:00–9:00pm	98-02 % of increase /decrease
ABC	1,438.5% ▲
CBS	73.4% ▼
FOX	45% ▲
NBC	38.9% ▲
UPN	176.8% ▲
WB	95.6% ▼
TOTAL	41% ▲

Source: TV Bloodbath: Violence on Prime Time A PTC State of the Television Industry Report www.parentstv.org

VIOLENCE DURING PRIME TIME
BROADCAST TELEVISION

9:00–10:00pm	98-02
	% of increase /decrease
ABC	451.6% ▲
CBS	30% ▼
FOX	175.5% ▲
NBC	57.6% ▼
UPN	4,976.9% ▲
WB	570% ▼
TOTAL	134.4% ▲

Source: TV Bloodbath: Violence on Prime Time A PTC State of the Television Industry Report www.parentstv.org

Things to Consider Before Giving to Television Charities or Ministries

You see starving kids on television, or someone knocks on your door. The needs are pressing and their stories are convincing. You reach for your checkbook, wallet, or credit card. STOP! First, sit down, take a deep breath, and think about what you're doing. Give wisely.

How does someone give wisely? A savvy consumer knows how to ask the right questions and do a little homework. The same precautions are essential before making donations. The following are some good questions to ask before you give:

Who wants your money? If you are unfamiliar with the charity, get its full name, address, and telephone number. Many organizations have names that are very similar to well-known charities. Ask whether the organization is listed as a tax exempt public charity by the IRS and whether your donation will be tax deductible.

How will they use your donation? A dramatic, heart-rending description of general need may get your attention, but you should know more before you give. Find out the substance of the appeal and the planned use of your money. For example, are the organization's main goals education and research, or service and distribution? If the organization's goal is public education, ask about their program in detail. Some direct mail educational campaigns achieve very good results and may be an appropriate use of your money. Be aware, however, that some organizations print a few facts in the fundraising literature they send to you and call the mailing and printing expenses the costs of public education.

What percentage would go toward true charitable purposes? Ask for written information that will show you a comparison of how much money the organization spends on administrative and fundraising fees and expenses versus how much it spends directly on the intended recipients or projects of the charity. You may want to compare the administrative costs, fees and expenses for several charities before deciding which charities to support.

Before giving, watch out for these red flags:

High Pressure Phone Calls: A legitimate charity will be glad to give you the time needed to check it out.

Prizes: Most honest charities do not try to entice you to give by telling you that you have won a prize when you haven't even entered a contest.

Avoidance of the U.S. Mail: Dishonest individuals usually try to avoid doing any business through the mail to avoid federal prosecution under postal statutes. Instead, they will insist on using a private courier service or picking up your check themselves.

What to keep in mind when giving:

Get information in writing from the charity before giving, including an annual report or other financial information. Do not give your credit card number out over the phone in response to a phone solicitation. Do not respond to letters that say you have pledged money unless you are certain that you did. Do not give cash. Write a check in the name of the charity, or if you are giving other property ask for a receipt. Consult an attorney before making a significant gift, whether making such a gift outright, by will, or by trust.

For More Information:

For charities that operate nationally, contact the Council of Better Business Bureau's Philanthropic Advisory Service at (703) 276-0100, the National Charities Information Bureau at (212) 929-6300, or the American Institute of Philanthropy at (301) 913-5200.

For local charities, organizations like your Better Business Bureau, chamber of commerce, or local chapter of the National Society of Fundraising Executives may also have information.

Source: Greg Abbott Attorney General of Texas 1-800 621-0508
http://www.oag.state.tx.us/AG_Publications/txts/charity.shtml

APPENDIX H

Percentages of Black and White Male Characters Shown in Different Guises		
	Black Male	White Male
Vulgar Profanity	70%	57%
Using Ungrammatical Language	52%	8%
Security Guard	45%	5%
Physical Violence	37%	45%
Hugged/Kissed	30%	18%
Non-Sexual Intimacy	22%	12%
Sexualized	19%	16%
Restrained or handcuffed	19%	2%
Sex	19%	19%
Caressed	15%	9%

Percentages of Black and White Female Characters Shown in Different Guises		
	Black Female	White Female
Sexualized	100%	60%
Vulgar Profanity	85%	19%
Hugged/Kissed	79%	55%
Physical Violence	58%	15%
Non-Sexual Intimacy	58%	26%
Restrained or handcuffed	58%	5%
Using Ungrammatical Language	42%	2%
Caressed	37%	22%
Sex	37%	3%
Security Guard	37%	0%

Source: The Black Image in The White Mind Robert M. Entman and Andrew Rojecki

NOTES

CHAPTER 1

1. Alex S. Jones, "Fox News Moves from the Margins to the Mainstream" citing a Pew Research Center study done in January 2002. The Pew Research Center is an independent opinion research group that studies attitudes toward the press, politics, and public policy issues. They are best known for regular national surveys that measure public attentiveness to major news stories, and for polling trends in values and fundamental political and social attitudes.

2. "In 2002, the U.S. media system is dominated by about ten transnational conglomerates including Disney, AOL Time Warner, News Corporation, Viacom, Vivendi Universal, Sony, Liberty, Bertelsmann, AT&T Comcast, and General Electric. Their media revenues range from roughly $8 billion to $35 billion per year. These firms tend to have holdings in numerous media sectors.AOL Time Warner, for example, ranks among the largest players in film production, recorded music, TV show production, cable TV channels, cable TV systems, book publishing, magazine publishing, and Internet service provision. This first tier owns all the commercial television networks, all the major Hollywood studios, four of the five firms that sell 90 percent of the music in the United States, a majority of the cable TV systems, all or part of most of the successful cable TV channels, and much, much more. Another twelve to fifteen firms, which do from $2 or $3 billion to $8 billion dollars per year in business, round out the system. Firms like Hearst, the

New York Times Company, the Washington Post Company, Cox, Advance, the Tribune Company, and Gannett tend to be less developed conglomerates, focusing on only two or three media sectors. All in all, these two dozen or so firms control the overwhelming percentage of movies, TV shows, cable systems, cable channels, TV stations, radio stations, books, magazines, newspapers, billboards, music and TV networks that constitute the media culture that occupies one-half of the average American's life."

CHAPTER 2

3. Neuromarketing research is also underway at Harvard Business School and Baylor College of Medicine, bringing "respectability" to this blatant effort at mind control coming soon to your television set.

CHAPTER 5

4. America's Second Harvest is the largest domestic hunger-relief organization in the United States. The America's Second Harvest mission is to feed hungry people by soliciting and distributing food and grocery products through a nationwide network of certified affiliate food banks and food-rescue programs and to educate the public about the nature of and solutions to the problem of hunger in America.

Suggested Readings

Amini, Fari, Richard Lannon, and Thomas Lewis. *A General Theory of Love*. New York: Random House, Inc. 2000.

Bagdikian, Ben H. *The Media Monopoly*. Boston, Mass.: Beacon Press, 2000.

Blumenthal, Howard J., and Oliver R. Goodenough. *The Business of Television*. New York: Billboard Books, 1991.

Bogle, Donald. *Primetime Blues: African Americans on Network Television*. New York: Farrar Straus & Giroux, 2001.

Chenoweth, Neil. *Rupert Murdoch: The Untold Story of the World's Greatest Media Wizard*. New York: Crown Business, 2002.

Garlington, Joseph L. *Worship: The Pattern of Things in Heaven*. Shippensburg, Pa.: Destiny Image Publishers, 1997.

Goldberg, Bernard. *Arrogance: Rescuing America from the Media Elite*. New York: Warner Books, Inc., 2003.

—————. *Bias: A CBS Insider Exposes How the Media Distort the News*. Washington, DC: Regnery Publishing Co., 2001.

Hack, Richard. *Clash of The Titans: How the Unbridled Ambition of Ted Turner and Rupert Murdoch Has Created Global Empires That Control What We Read and Watch*. Beverly Hills: New Millennium Press, 2003.

Johnston, Robert K. *Reel Spirituality: Theology and Film in Dialogue*. Grand Rapids, Mich.: Baker Academic, 2000.

Medved, Michael, and Diane Medved, Ph.D. *Saving Childhood*. Grand Rapids, Mich.: Zondervan Publishing House, 1998.

Rampton, Sheldon, and John Stauber. *Weapons of Mass Deception: The Uses of Propaganda in Bush's War on Iraq*. New York: J.P. Tarcher/Penguin Group, 2003.

Solomon, Jerry, ed. *Arts, Entertainment & Christian Values: Probing the Headlines That, Impact Your Family*. Grand Rapids, Mich.: Kregel Publications, 2000.

BIBLIOGRAPHY

Anthony, Ole. "Televangelist Investigations: Corruption in Televangelism and Paganism in the American Church." Speech. 23 September 1994. www.trinityfi.org/trinity/investi.html.

Bakker, Jim. *I Was Wrong*. Nashville, Tenn.: Thomas Nelson, Inc., 1996.

Entman, Robert M., and Andrew Rojecki, *The Black Image in the White Mind: Media and Race in America*. Chicago: University of Chicago Press, 2001.

"Food Advertising Strategies." Student Handout. Media Awareness Network. www.media-awareness.ca.

Frazao, Elizabeth, ed. "America's Eating Habits: Changes and Consequences." *Agriculture Information Bulletin* 750. Washington, DC: Economic Research Service, US Department of Agriculture, May 1999. www.ers.usda.gov/publications/aib750.

Gibbs, A.P. *Worship: The Christian's Highest Occupation*. Kansas City, Kans.: Walterick Publishers, 1950.

"Giving to Charities." Attorney General of Texas Greg Abbott web site. www.oag.state.tx.us/AG_Publications/txts/charity.shtml.

Huesmann, L. Rowell, Jessica Moise-Titus, Cheryl-Lynn Podolski, and Leonard D. Eron. "Longitudinal Relations Between Children's Exposure to TV Violence and TheirAggressive and Violent Behavior in Young Adulthood: 1997-1992." *Developmental Psychology* 39, 2 (2003): 203.

Jones, Alex S. "Fox News Moves from the Margins to the Mainstream." *The New York Times*, 1 December 2002.

Kenoly, Ron, and Dick Bernal. *Lifting Him Up: How You Can Enter Into Spirit-Led Praise and Worship*. Lake Mary, Fla.: Creation House, 1995.

McChesney, Robert W. *Rich Media, Poor Democracy: Communication Politics in Dubious Times*. New York: The New Press, 2000.

McChesney, Robert W., and John Nichols. *Our Media, Not Theirs: The Democratic Struggle Against Corporate Media*. New York: Seven Stories Press, 2002.

McKenzie, Vashti. *Journey to the Well*. Chicago: Urban Ministries, Inc., 2002.

McLuhan, Marshall. *Understanding Media: The Extensions of Man*. Cambridge,Mass.: MIT Press, 1994.

Murray, David, Joel Schwartz, and S. Robert Lichter. *It Ain't Necessarily So: How Media Make and Unmake the Scientific Picture of Reality*. New York: Penguin Putnam Inc., 2002.

Newman, Jay. *Religion vs. Television: Competitors in Cultural Context*. Westport, Conn.: Praeger Publishers, 1996.

Nord, Mark, Margaret Andrews, and Steven Carlson. "Household Food Security in the United States, 2002." *Food Assistance and Nutrition Research Report* FANRR35. Washington, DC: Economic Research Service, US Department of Agriculture, October 2003. www.ers.usda.gov/publications/fanrr35.

Peers, Martin. "Buddy, Can You Spare Some Time?" *The Wall Street Journal*, 26 January 2004, B1.

Postman, Neil. *Amusing Ourselves to Death: Public Discourse in the Age of Show Business*. New York: Viking Press, 1985.

Richmond, Ray. "Cuisine Scene." *The Hollywood Reporter*, 18-24 November, 2003. S-4.

Rigby, Neville. "U.S. Exports Bad Diets." *USA Today*, 5 February 2004, A.14.

Stanley, Andy. *Visioneering: God's Blueprint for Developing and Maintaining Vision*. Sisters, Oreg.: Multnomah Publishers, Inc., 2001.

Stone, Bryan P., Faith and Film Theological Themes at the Cinema. St. Louis, Mo.: Chalice Press, 2000.

"TV Bloodbath: Violence on Prime Time Broadcast TV: A PTC State of the Television Industry Report." Report. Parents Television Council. www.parentstv.org.

Wells, Melanie. "In Search of the Buy Button." *Forbes*, September 2003, 62-70.